HILARIOUS HUNTING CARTOONS

HILARIOUS HUNTING CARTOONS

John Troy
Color by Doris Troy

Foreword by Nick Lyons

Skyhorse Publishing

Skyhorse Publishing books may be purchased in bulk at special discounts for sales promotion, corporate gifts, fund-raising, or educational purposes. Special editions can also be created to specifications. For details, contact the Special Sales Department, Skyhorse Publishing, 307 West 36th Street, 11th Floor, New York, NY 10018 or info@skyhorsepublishing.com.

Skyhorse® and Skyhorse Publishing® are registered trademarks of Skyhorse Publishing, Inc.®, a Delaware corporation.

Visit our website at www.skyhorsepublishing.com.

10 9 8 7 6 5 4 3 2 1

Library of Congress Cataloging-in-Publication Data

Troy, John.

Hilarious hunting cartoons / John Troy ; color by Doris Troy ; with a foreword by Nick Lyons.

p.   cm.

ISBN-13: 978-1-60239-305-9 (alk. paper)

1. Hunting in art. 2. American wit and humor, Pictorial. I. Title.

NC1429.T695A4 2007b

741.5'6973—dc22

2007020065

Cover design by Adam Bozarth
Cover image credit: John Troy

Print ISBN: 978-1-5107-3224-7
Ebook ISBN: 978-1-5107-3229-2

Printed in China

To Doris,
my wife, my life

FOREWORD

Hunting bears these resemblances to fishing: it is the pursuit of a natural creature, it is often practiced by passionate enthusiasts, and it provides fields full of fodder for the shrewd humorist. In prose, no one has matched the late and brilliant Ed Zern; but John Troy has for decades made cartoons that consistently find the hilarity in a sport that some consider merely a killing field.

The humorist punctures the pretensions, the illusions, the passions of folk oblivious to the ironies of their actions, the way they look to others not so addicted; the humorist shows how logical (if absurd) extensions or exaggerations of what a class of people do can illuminate their foibles.

Thus, in a cartoon by Troy, a man sets up a tree seat and rungs on the wall of his living room, dresses with cap and coat for hunting, with a rifle across his legs and a thermos in his hand, and his wife, having tea with friends, says, "Deer season never really ends for Edwin."

Thus, two hunters on a log, pelted by squirrels in the wrong time of year, wonder when the squirrel season will open.

Thus, a hunter has called in a bear, a giraffe, a cobra, and assorted other creatures, and his pal wisely says, "Let me see that duck call, Al."

A dog, Spot, insists on going in the direction opposite that in which some mighty big paw prints are headed, and a deer in camouflage stands against a tree directly behind a camouflaged hunter looking elsewhere.

All is fair game to the cartoonist—and John Troy misses no opportunity to find humor in what thousands of hunters will recognize as their daily routine, served up slantwise, hilariously.

—Nick Lyons

ACKNOWLEDGMENTS

This book of cartoons owes its life to the many publishers, editors, art directors, and art editors who throughout my life bought my cartoons. Their wisdom is measured by each laugh we shared, sometimes thousands of miles apart. I thank you, deeply.

—JOHN TROY

INTRODUCTION

This book of hunting cartoons began its life sixty-four years ago, when I was ten. You'll find many of your hunting pals and hunting dogs in this chronicle of hunting humor.

Each cartoon tells a story, and being a cartoon, the humorous side of each story. Like the time I fell through the ice on a bitter cold winter day. My hunter pals pulled me out, all the while laughing their heads off. Red drove me home in his Model-A Ford with no windows, the fourteen-degree weather soon encasing me in icy armor. Now that's funny.

You'll see yourself, too, in dozens of these cartoons, and even if you don't, your buddies will.

One thing a hunter finds out early in his hunting years is that a hound is smarter than he is, and much hunting lore revolves around this reality.

I spent my early years being trained by numerous dogs, some good, some bad. . . .

My Uncle John let me borrow his old double-barrel and hunting dog one day when I was about fourteen or fifteen. A slight rain was falling. I knew the rabbits would be out, and Butchie, a middle-sized combination wire-haired white-and-grey spotted dog, was my tutor for the day. A short hike found me in the local hayfields. Butchie would chase anything that moved, and pretty soon he had rabbits running hither and yon, and I missed every one! What Butchie taught me that day was that rabbits, to stay dry, lay under fallen leaves. He jumped one after another, until I ran out of shells.

I had a beagle once, named Suzie, and like Butchie, she spent most of her time afield pursuing anything that moved. She'd snooze in my lap at lunchtime or anytime I rested. After a long hunt I'd pack her out in my game pocket. She had a special bark for squirrels, a woo-woo for rabbits, a high pitched yap-yap-yap for pheasant, and so on. When she finally taught me everything she thought I could handle, we made a good pair. If we hunted a spot more than once she just knew which way the rabbit would run, or the direction the grouse would flush.

So you'll find a lot of dog cartoons in this book and none of them ridicule the hunting dog. My pal Suzie is long gone, but I still hear her in the fields, or catch a glimpse of her in the twilight shadow of the cedars. And I remember the fun we used to have, so I draw a cartoon of us.

These are our stories, in cartoons. Don't be surprised if you discover that many are your stories, too.

—JOHN TROY

HILARIOUS HUNTING CARTOONS

"Deer season never really ends for Edwin."

"When does squirrel season open?"

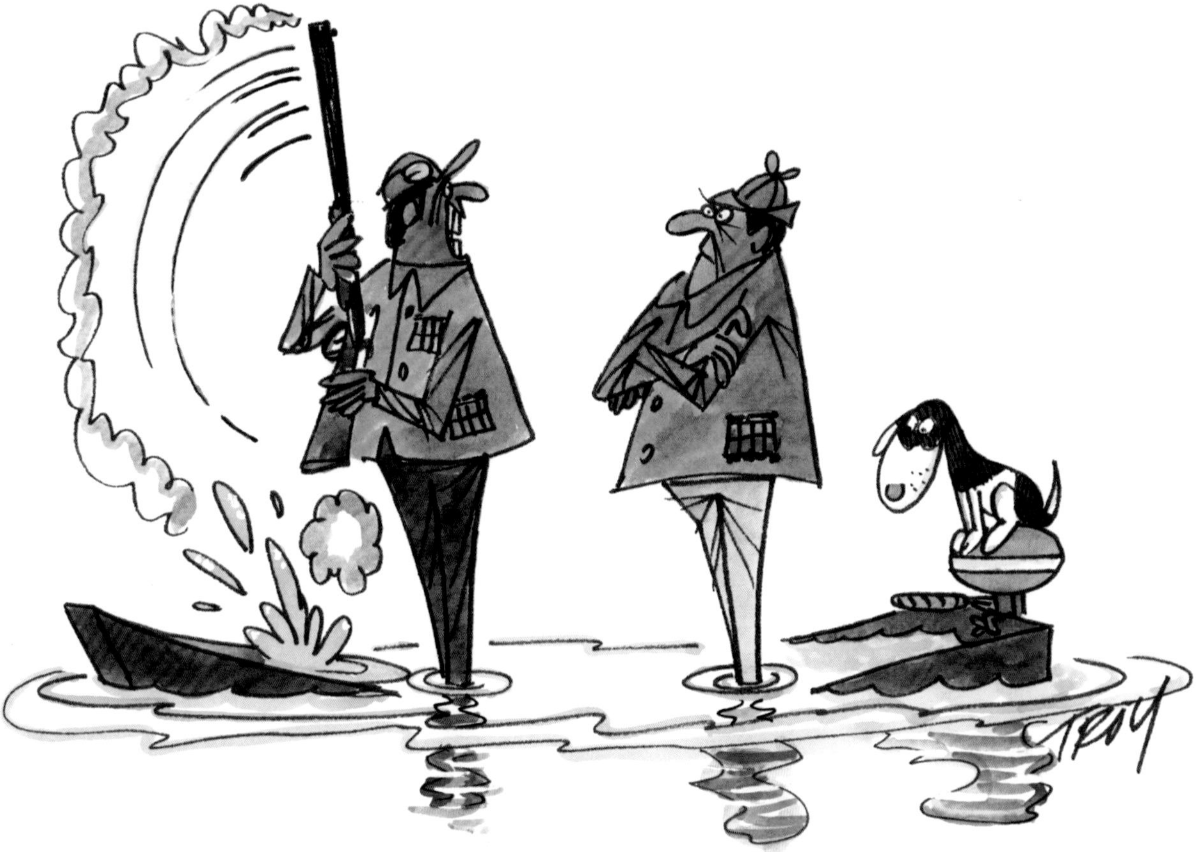

“Oh, I see, it’s point the gun *up* for safety.”

"Are you going on a trip, or retrieving a duck?"

"I'm sure glad I thought to take you hunting, Spot."

"See that? He's not gun-shy at all."

"I'll keep the light on."

"It looks like your dog is an overachiever, Al."

"I'll be darned—there is something on my shoulder!"

"He's either hit a hot trail already, or someone's opened a lunchbox in the parking lot."

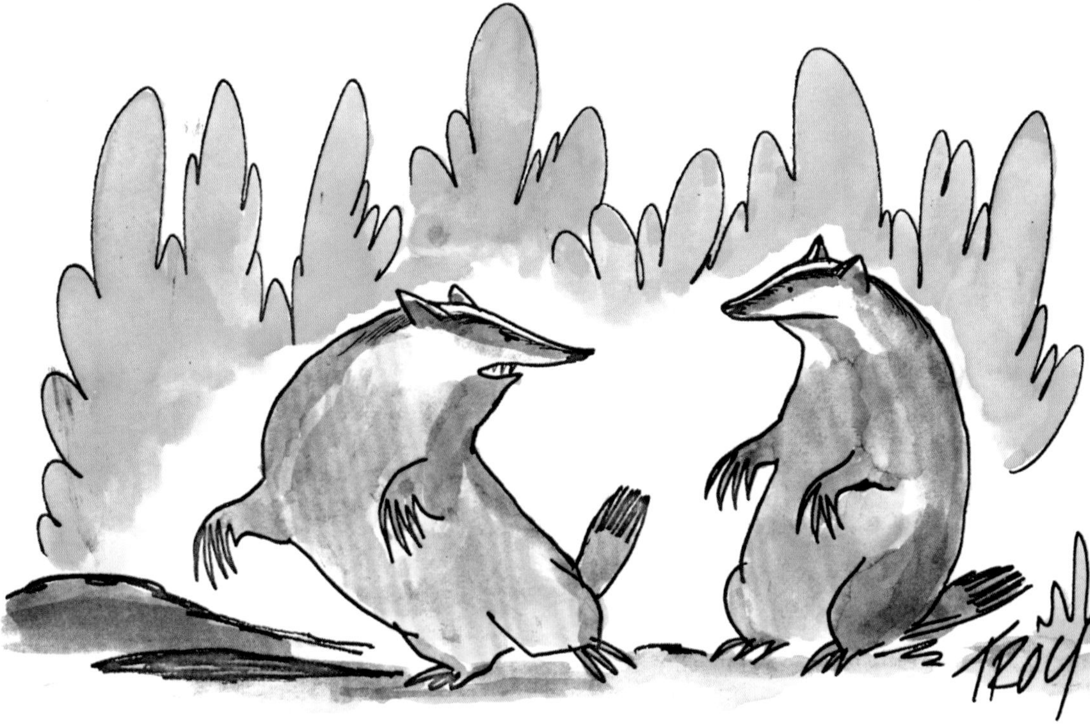
TROY

"Stop badgering me!"

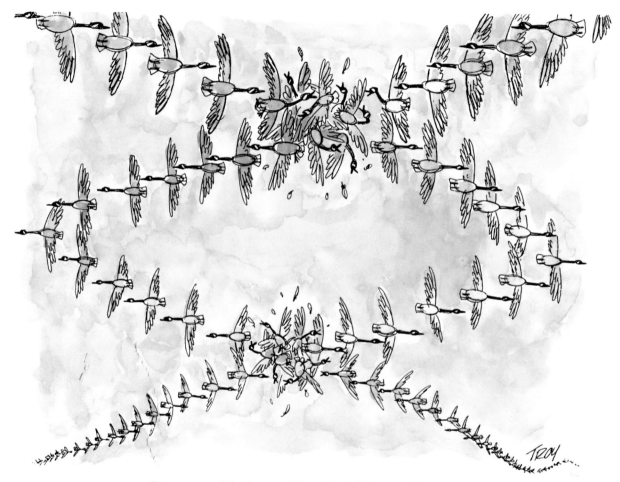

"Excuse me." "Whoops!" "My fault." "Sorry!" "You first."
"Pardon me." "Sorry." "S'cuse me." "Look out!" "Pardon . . ."

"Training school, here we come again!"

"Take my word for it—they're easier to retrieve *after* I shoot!"

"Spot, fishing season is over. Retrieve the *duck*!"

"Trying to poach our decoy, huh? Hmm, this is a tough call."

"And Baby Bear said, 'This one is just right.'"

"So that's how they know which way north is."

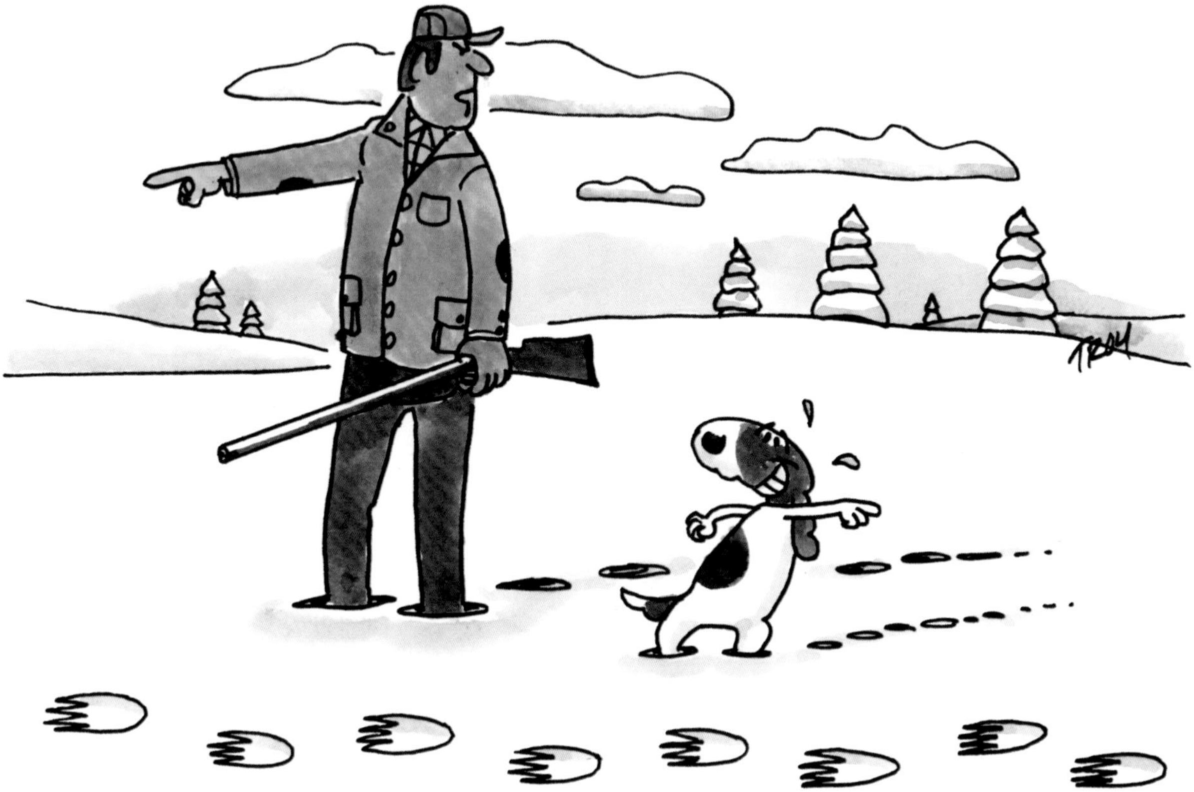

"No, Spot, this way!!"

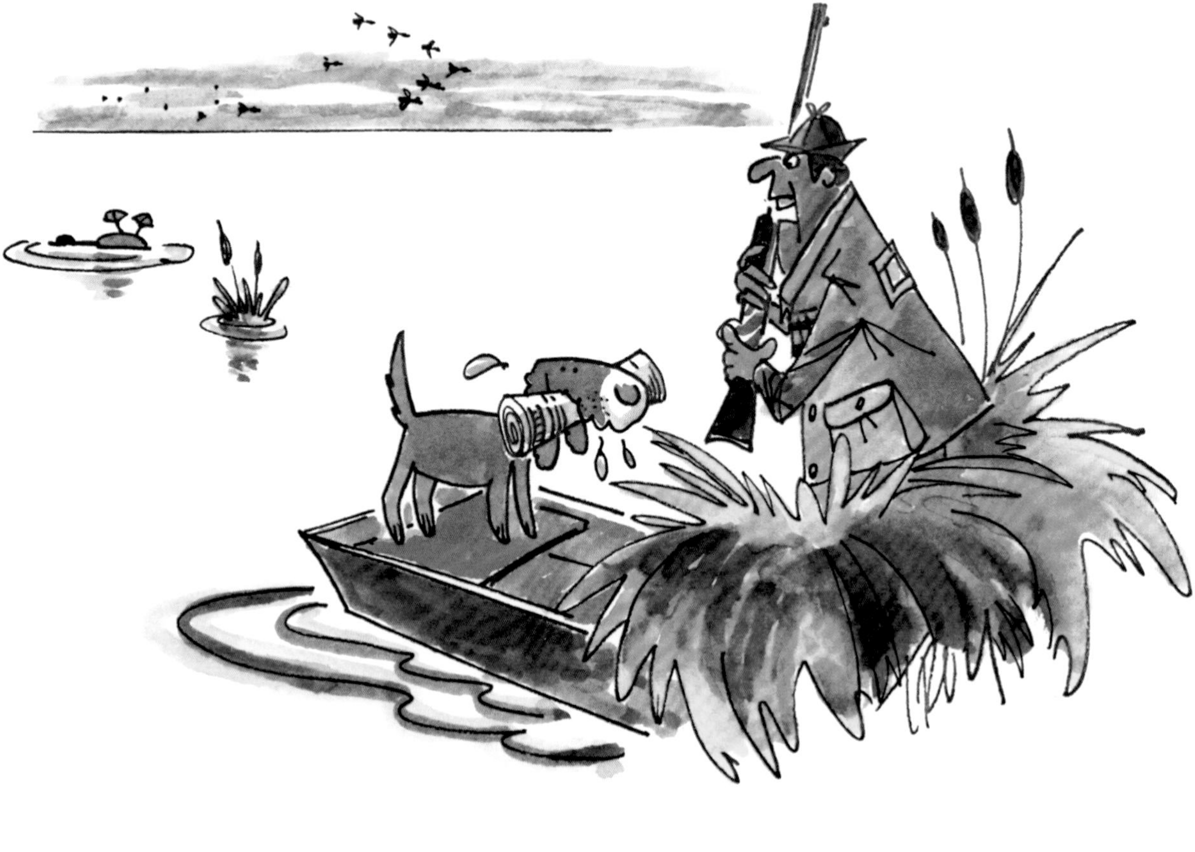

“No, no, you idiot—the duck!”

"Spot, go find a safe place and sit."

"Could you at least diet until your feet hit the ground!?"

"That's a heckuva nice trophy, Al."

"No, no, not cocoon hat, *raccoon hat.* R-A-C-C-O-O-N!"

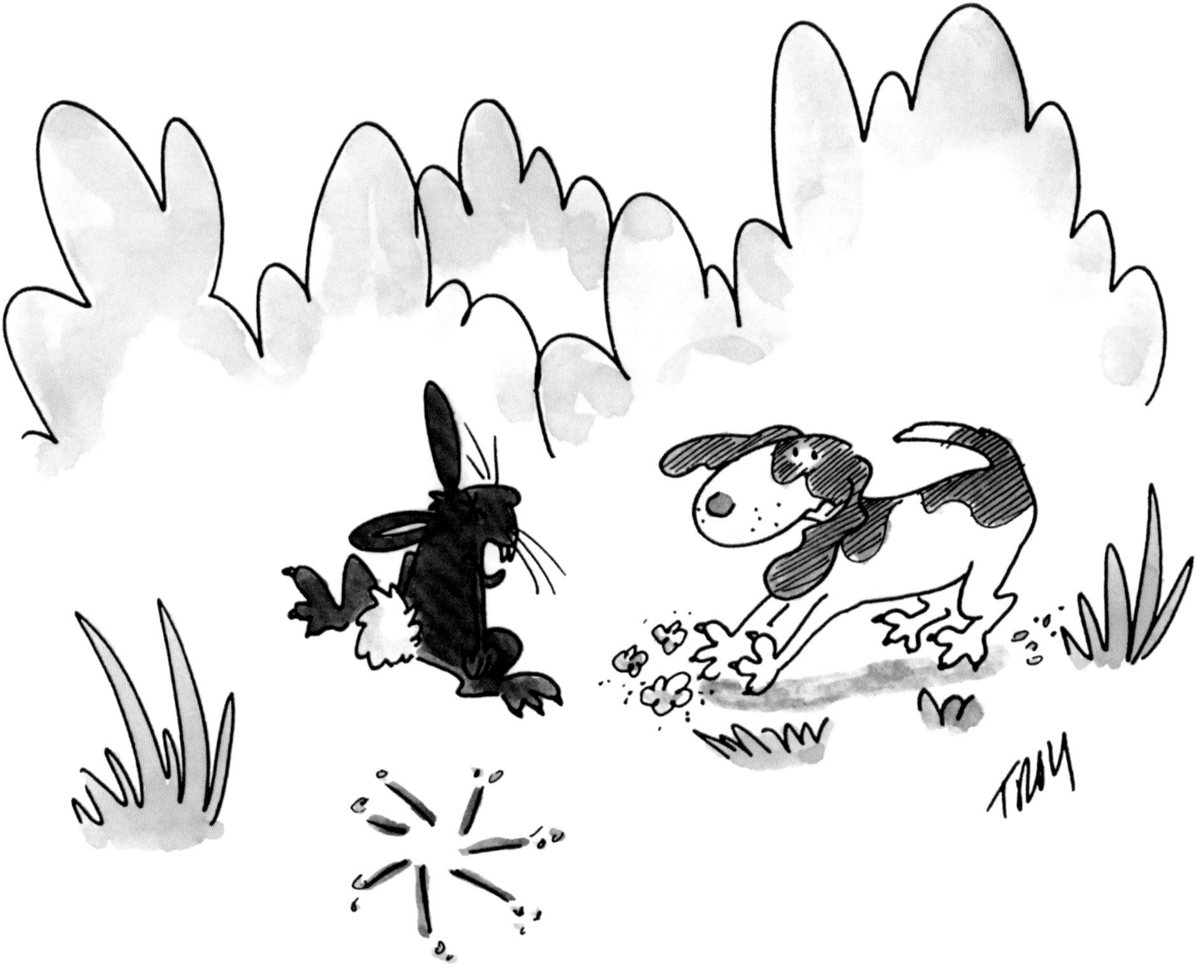

“STOP HOUNDING ME!”

"I don't think our 'coon dogs are aggressive enough."

"Yup, Spot is all nose. Case in point."

"Do you want to be in shape for opening day, or don't you?"

"Spot, stop barking 'treed' so we can all go home!"

"Why can't you just point like other dogs?"

"I'll be darn glad when your cold is gone."

"He gets homesick otherwise."

"It's a first aid kit, and if you ever hunted with Spot, you wouldn't ask."

"And what, may I ask, motivated you to become an environmentalist?"

"The first yahoo that says, 'Did you get your buck?' gets a load of buckshot!"

"Oh, my sleeve? Something on my sleeve? Which one? The right one?
No? Oh, I see. The left one. Ahhh . . ."

"I think I'll lighten up on Spot's high-protein diet."

"He said this is the first time he's ever been confused for more than a week."

"Takes his work seriously, doesn't he?"

"You better have a darn good reason for being gone so long!"

"In dog years I'm 280 years old. Hunting with you, I feel it."

"Did you say 'off-the-road' or 'off-the-ground' vehicle?"

"Yessir, been deer hunting for nigh on forty years. Ain't nuthin' I don't know about—Say, don't I know you from somewhere?"

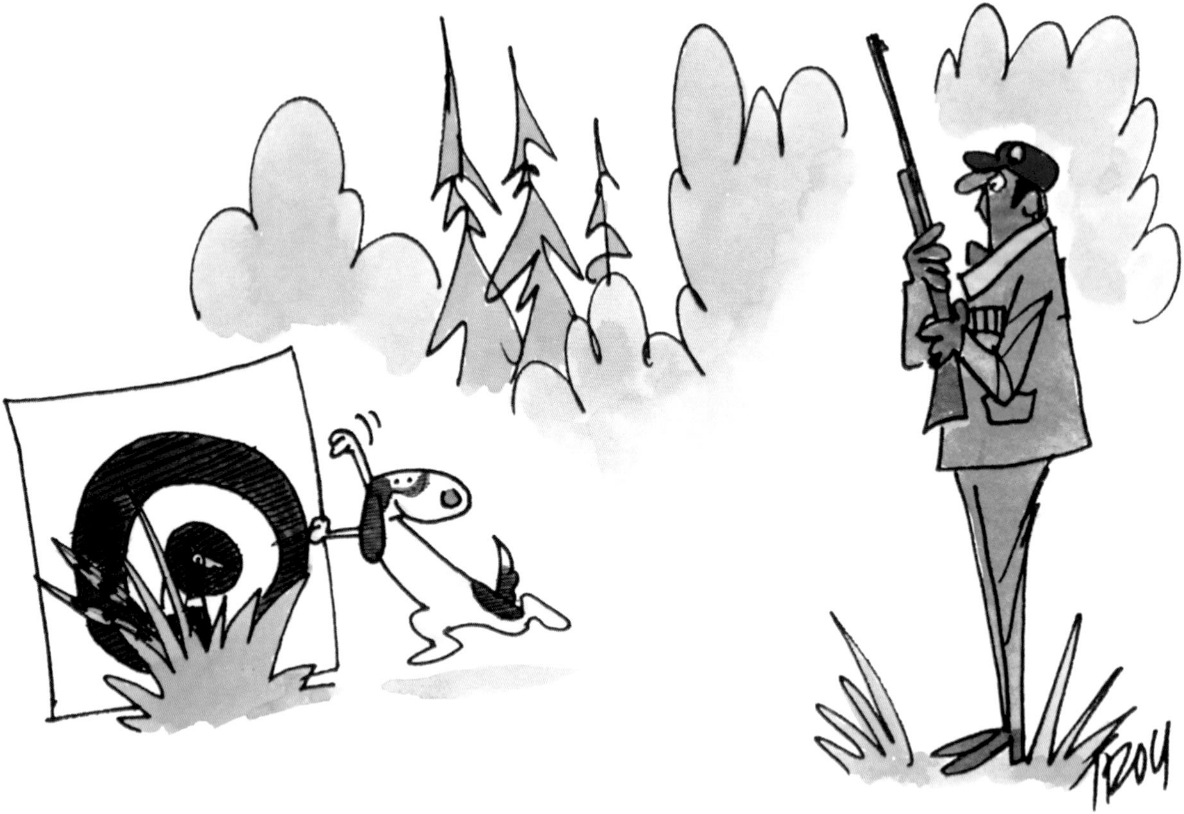
TROY

"KNOCK IT OFF!"

"That's four million one hundred and eighty straight misses, Mr. Fenson. Your shooting has gone all to hell."

"Ah, the best part of hunting—a hot cup of coffee, a quiet moment . . ."

" 'It ain't the size of the dog in the fight but the size of the fight in the dog'
just won't cut it today, old boy."

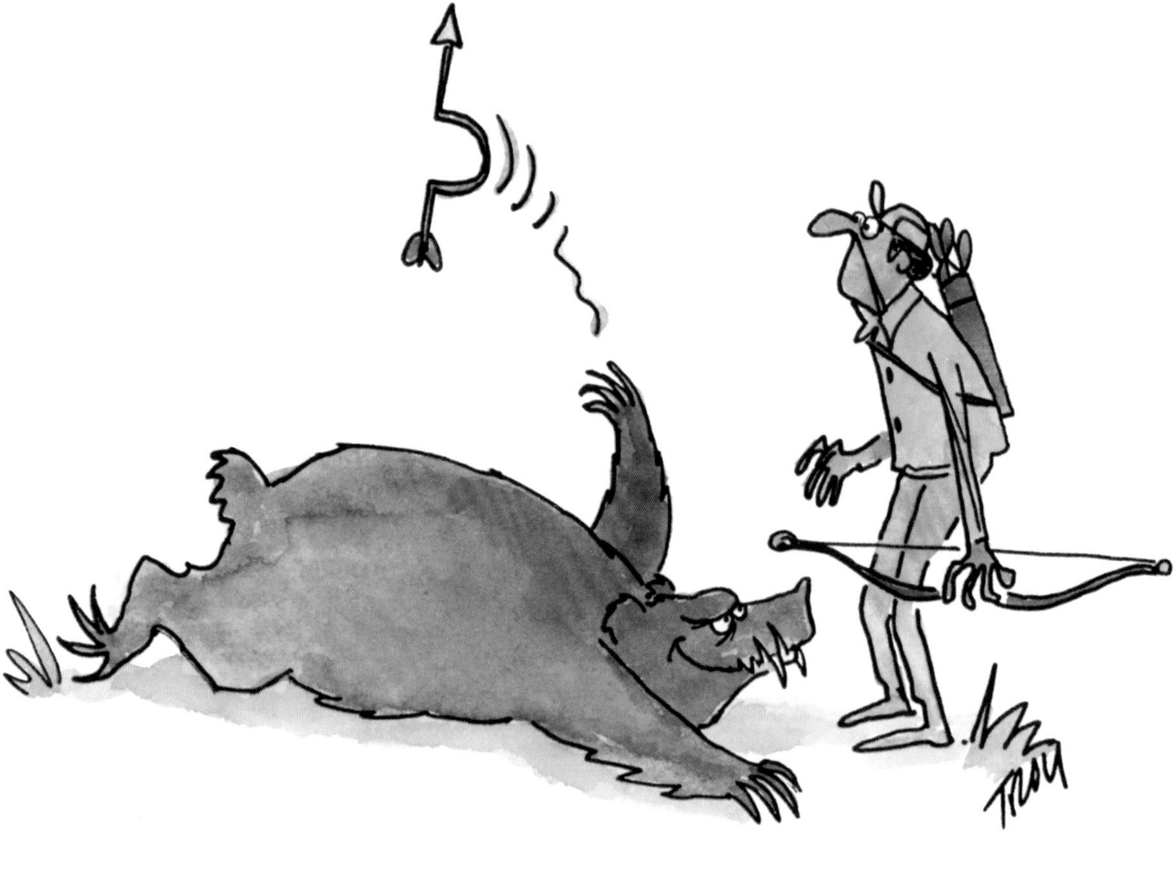

"Let me see that duck call, Al."

"This is the last time I sign up for your 'economy' elephant hunt!"

"We're going hunting, Spot, not to the mall!"

"How about pointing them while they're still on the ground?"

"I don't care how many pheasants are in that bush—*move it!*"

"Just point, I'll do the counting!"

"Okay, Spot, you can run faster than a pheasant. *Now do you mind flushing it?*"

"*You* tell him he can't be our leader."

"Pierre, I have been thinking about going into real estate lately."

"When Spot hunts rabbits, you need a shotgun *and* a shovel!"

"So far, it hasn't been a very good season."

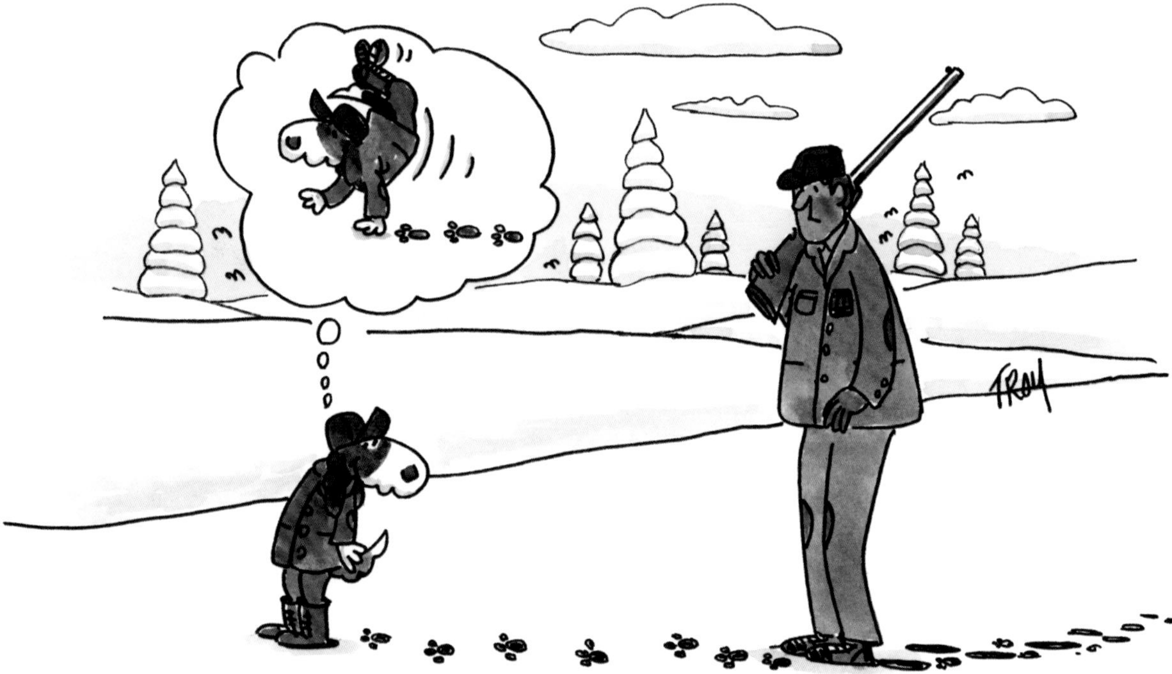
TROM

"So, how long do bears hibernate?"

"No, Spot, the season opens at eight o'clock. *That's* when I turn you loose."

"Your father is a real turkey."

"See if I take *you* hunting again!"

"Uh-oh, February . . . No hunting, no fishing. It's straightjacket time."

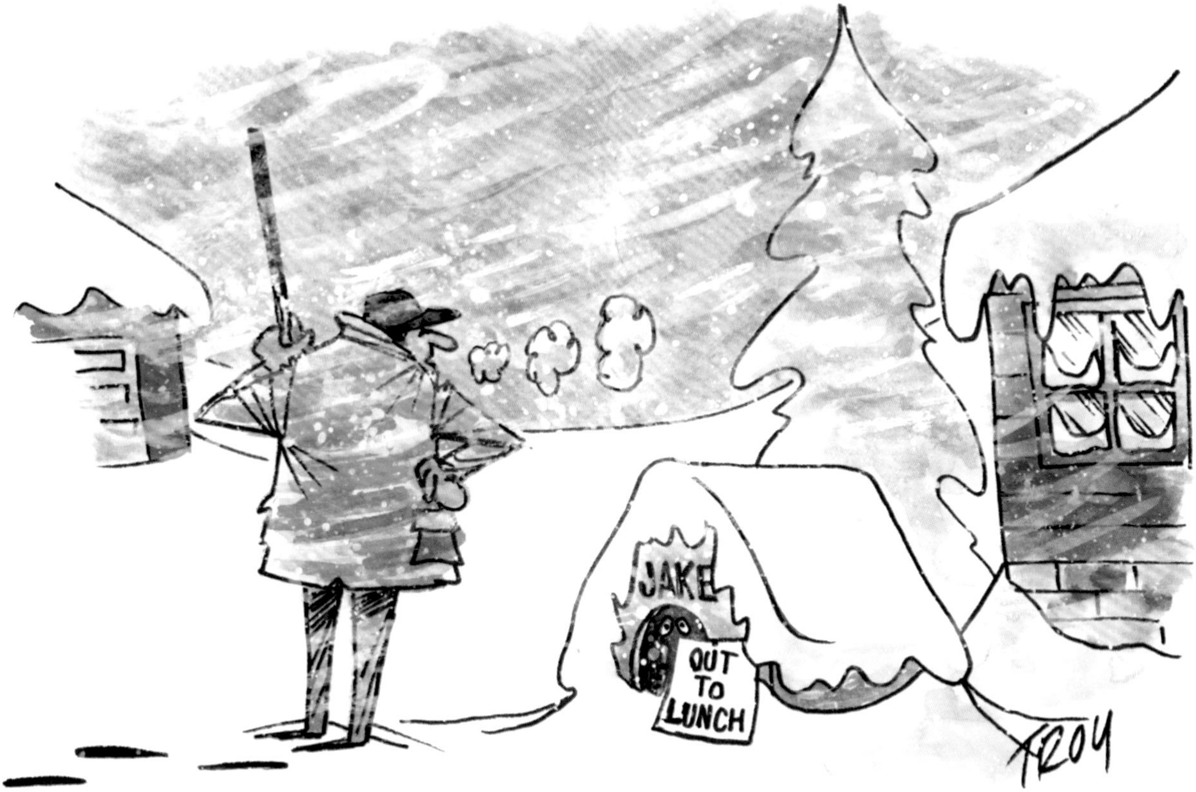
JAKE
OUT TO LUNCH
TROY

"Fair weather friend!"

"I know the snow is cold, Spot, but that's not what earmuffs are for."

"We're electing a new leader; pass it on." "We're electing a new leader; pass it on." "We're electing a . . ."

"Sure, that's a question I often ask myself: 'Do I want to be overpopulated and starve to death, or blown mercifully away by a 30-06 magnum rifle?'"

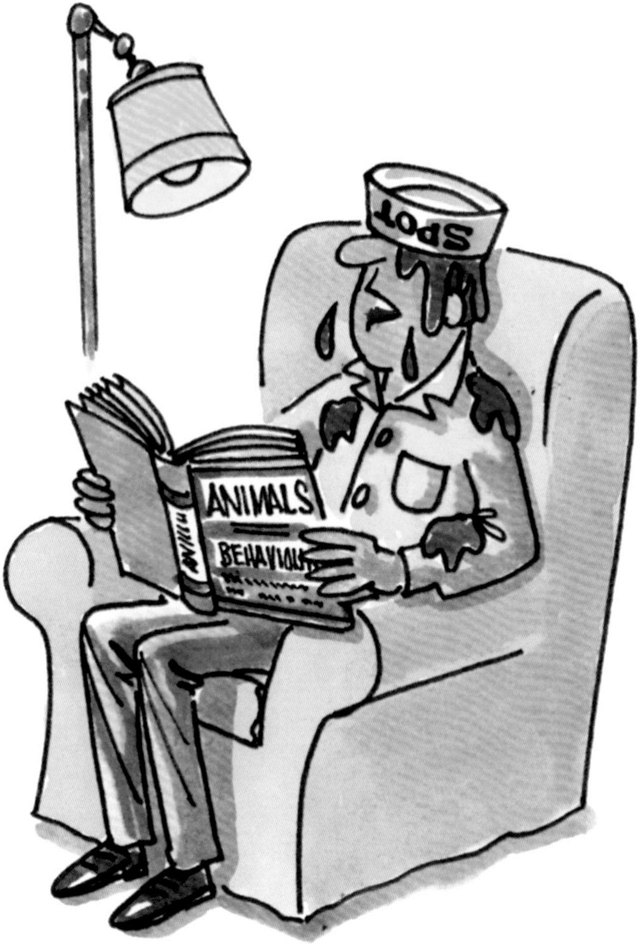
SPOT
ANIMALS

“It says here that pigs are emotionally more stable than dogs and . . . Nice Spot. Real mature, Spot.”

"Why don't you develop cabin fever and go out for a run?"

"Funny, even with you helping, this canoe gets heavier and heavier."

"Did your shooting improve, dear?"

"We better start thinking diet."

"Well, so much for lambs being easy prey for us eagles."

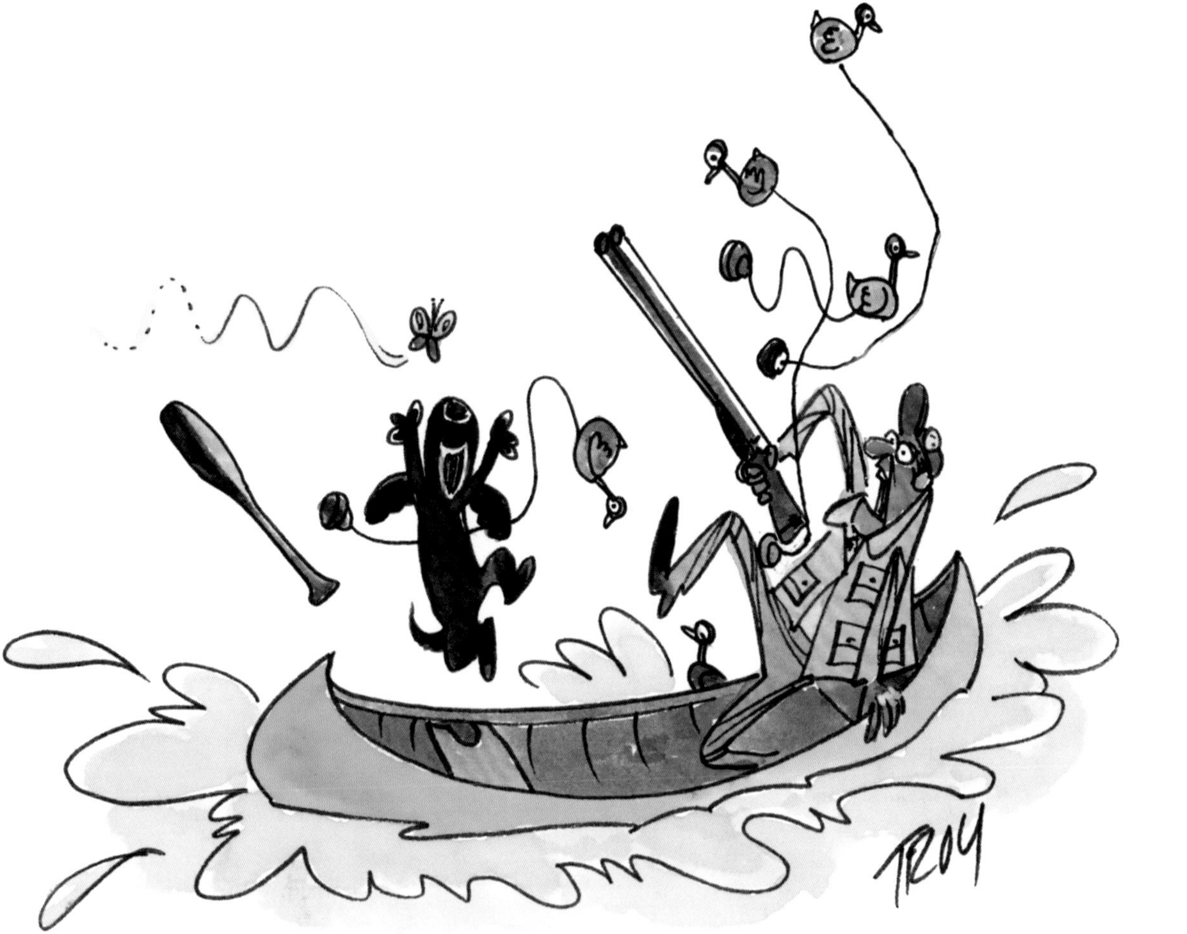
TROY

“Sit! Sit!”

"Yup, Spot fills a void in my life. Luckily, my medical insurance covers it."

"I'll be darn glad when hunting season is over."

"Play dead—it's our only chance."

"*Retrieve*, Spot, means 'to find and bring back,' not 'to find and eat out'!"

"*YOU* tell him to retrieve the duck."

"What is it you're chasin', Spot? A rabbit, pheasant, quail . . . ?"

"All right, can the commenting and get that duck!"

"That time of the year, eh Spot? Don't know whether to go hunting or fishing?"

"Nice growing old with you, eh Spot? Just didn't think it would be today."

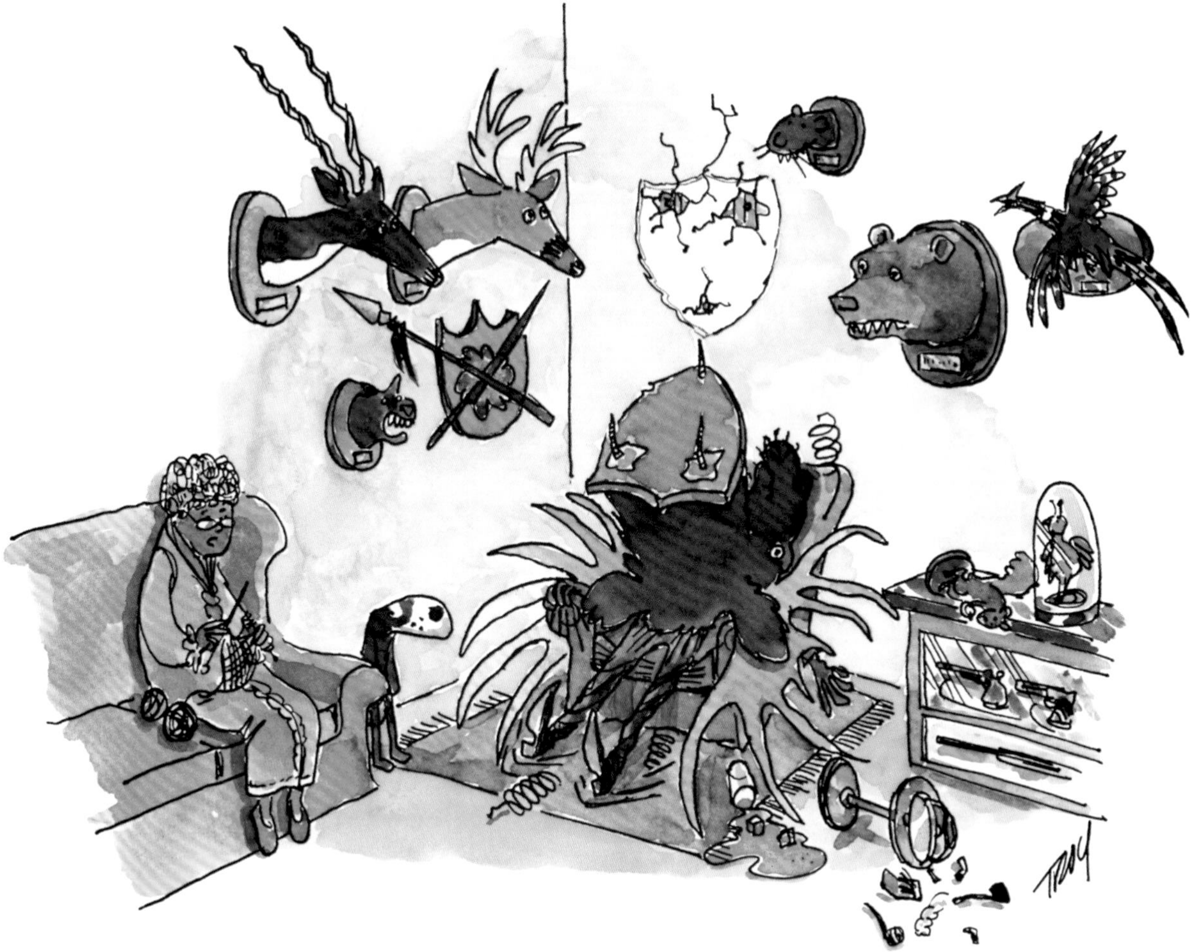
TROY

"Serves you right."

"Heck, I shoot wardens on sight . . . You're a warden?! Like I say, I shoot warthogs on sight—did that sound like *warden* to you? Heh, heh. Well, like I was saying, I been hunting warthogs since I was knee high . . ."

"I'm not what you would call a really good shot."

"Edmund's only link to the great outdoors is the hunting channel."

"Well, I've got the 'mating call' down pat. Now how's the 'get lost' call go?"

"That look of sheer terror? No, not a bear—left his lunch in the car again."

"I'll bet you can't wait for trout season."

"Your gun appears to be throwing what I like to call a 'donut pattern.'"

"Okay, Spot, let's see if those big bucks I spent taught you how to hunt close . . . Spot? . . . Spot!"

"The good news is, Mr. Filmore, this is heaven. The bad news is, this is posted property."

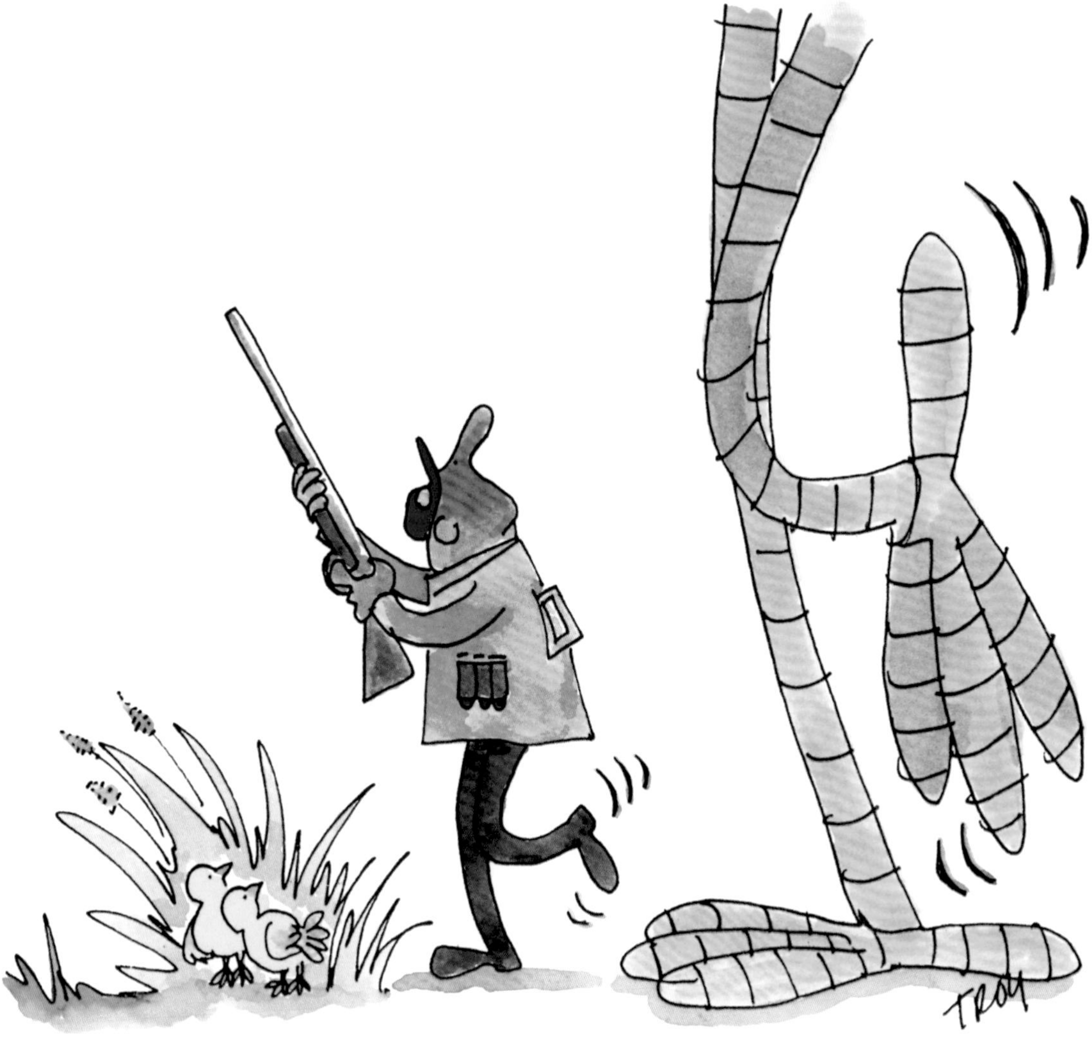
TROY

"Never saw a rabbit run such a wide circle."

"Here they come—look alive now!"

"My insurance doesn't cover me when I hunt with Spot."

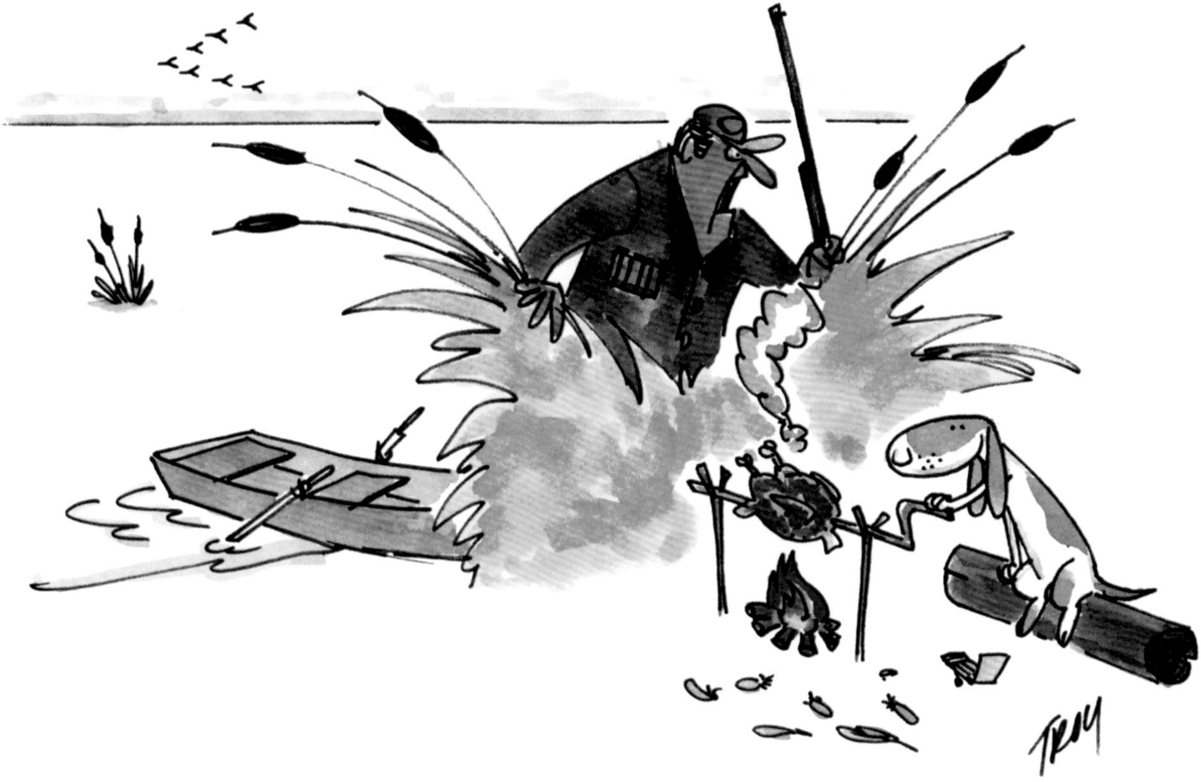

"AHA!"

TROY

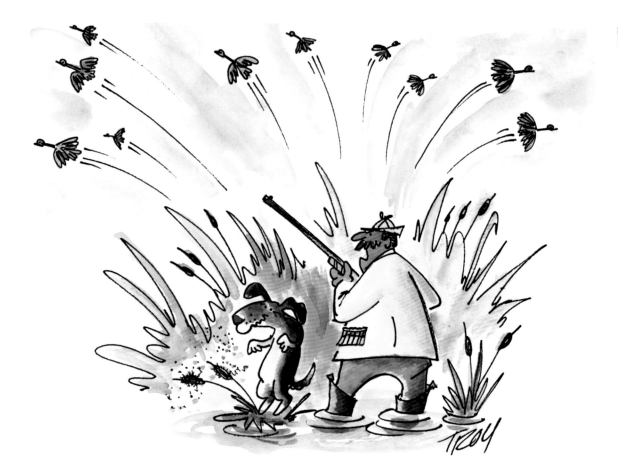

“Gesundheit.”

"Best duck hunter in the county. Sure like to know what his secret is."

"That's my accountant—he figures out my points total on ducks."

"This is a heck of a way to start the duck season."

"He's a good retriever, but has a confidence problem."

"Retrieving would be easier, Spot, if you took those three tennis balls out of your mouth."

"You have to admire his style."

"What do you mean retired? You're only *four years old*!"

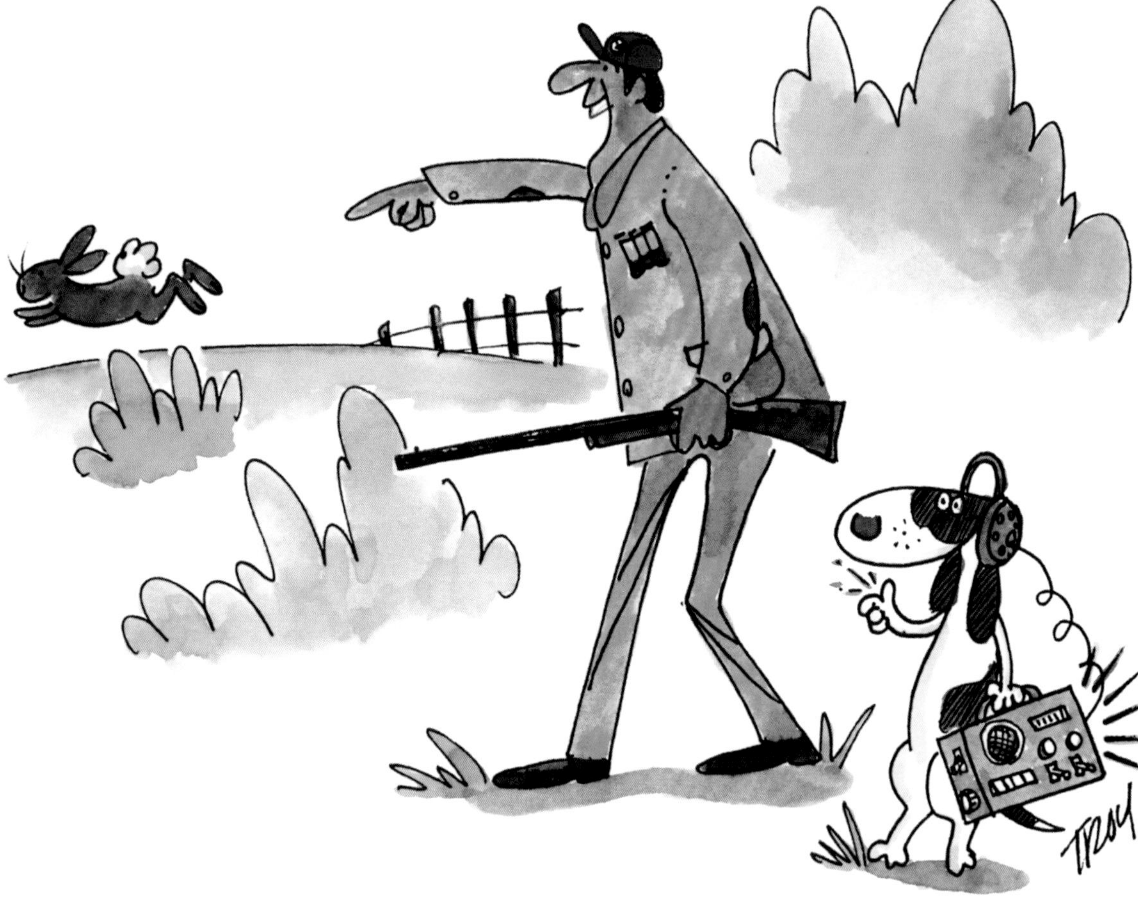
TROY

"Trail, boy, trail!"

"Wonderful, Spot, now any bright ideas how *I* get over?"

"Are you sure he's run rabbits before?"

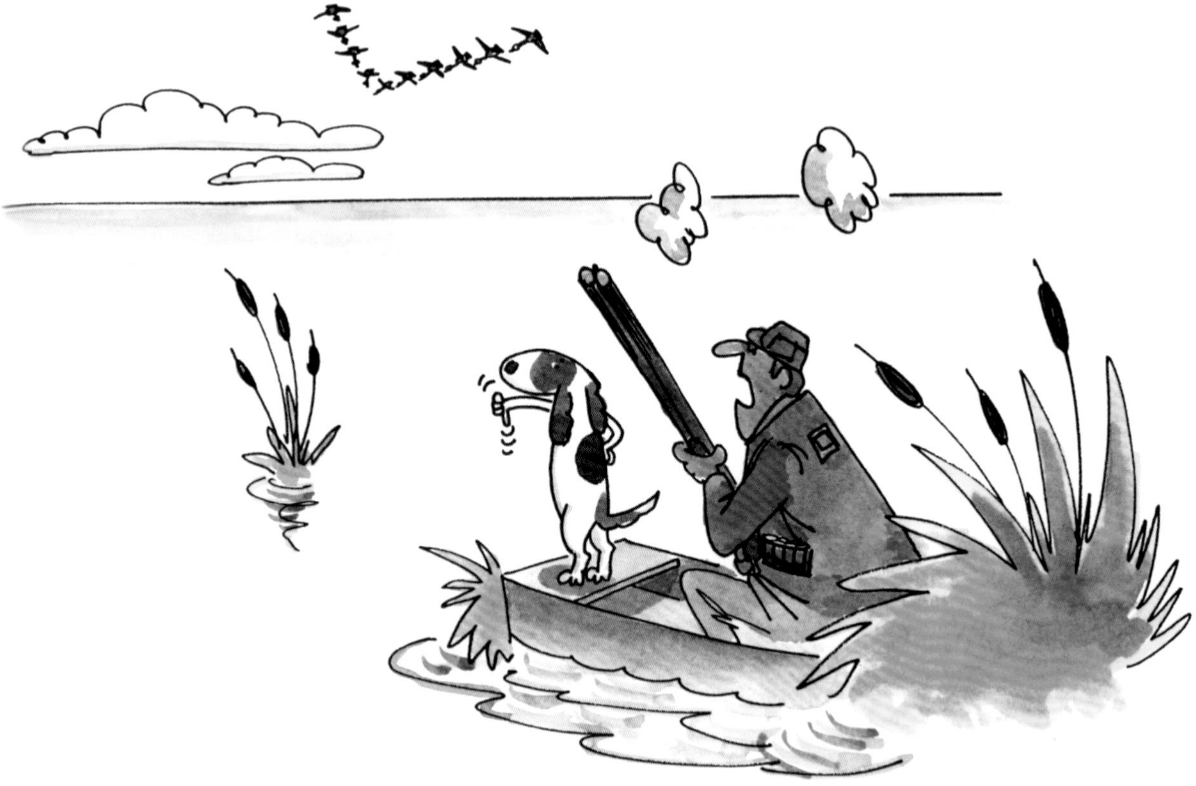

"I know I missed!"

"Where is it, Spot? What is it? Pheasant? Grouse? Rabbit?"

"Your gun is throwing a doughnut pattern, Ed, and it looks like both barrels, too."

"Spot is really catching on to retrieving. All we have to do now is get him to do it in our direction."

"This is your guide—be sure to feed him."

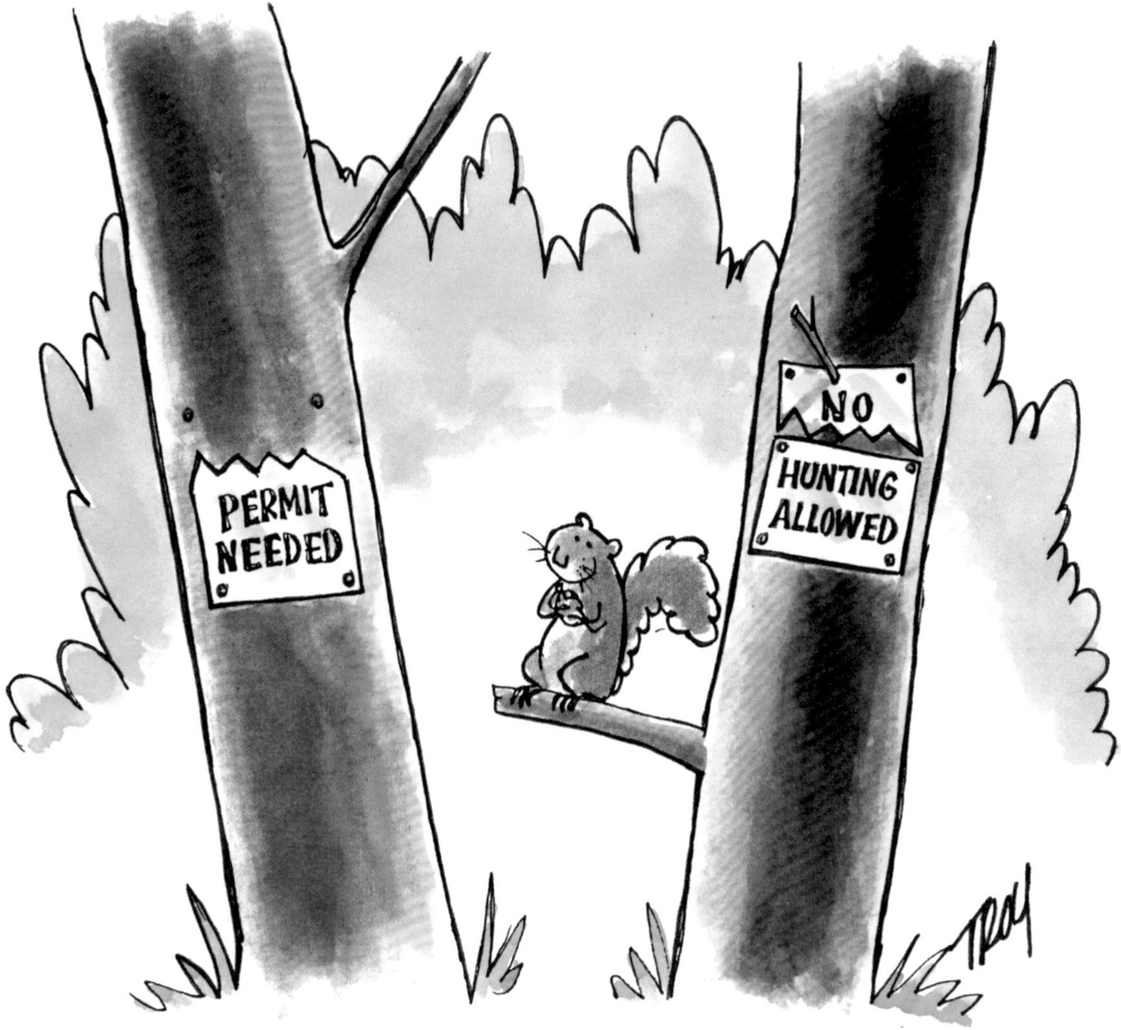

PERMIT
NEEDED
NO
HUNTING
ALLOWED
TROY

"Somebody's got their cold feet on me. *All four of them!*"

"Now that hunting season is over, I'd suggest separate vacations."

"Yissir, son, bow season is dangerous, so be careful you don't trip over any of these arrows."

"The next time, bring *both* your skis!"

"Guess who made some new friends while we were hunting?"

"And here's a handy little item that goes nicely with your combination hunting and fishing license."

"Edmund has trouble hitting a moving target."

"Buford, you're a disgrace to the National Park Service.
You're supposed to arrest poachers, not eat them!"

"He always manages to stay in shape during the off-season."

"I'm going hunting with Spot tomorrow—it reminded me to make out my living will."

"What do you mean 'It's time to get hunting?' It's two o'clock in the morning!"

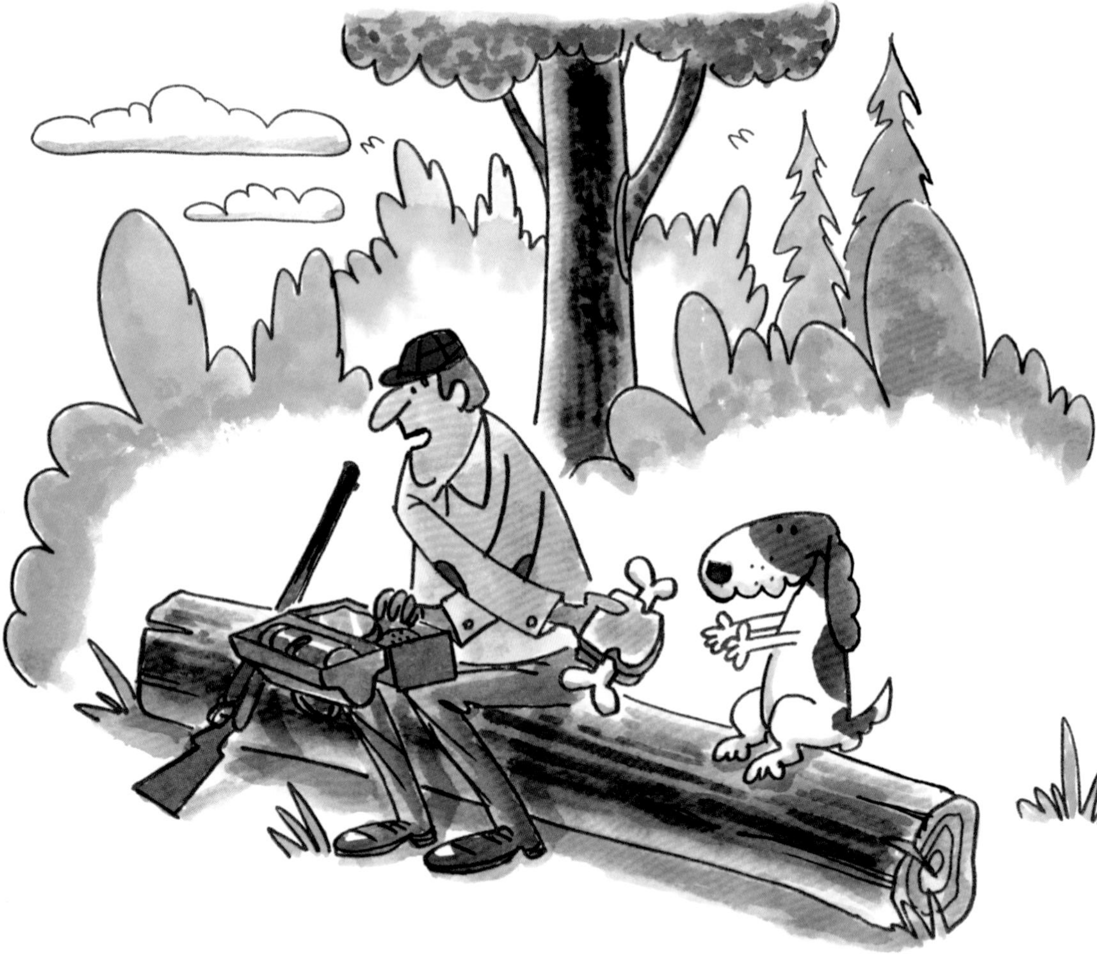

"Yours?"

"I don't think hunting and your ballet lessons are a good mix, Spot."

"He's been a different dog since he saw the Olympics on TV."

"Uh-oh, it looks like we're going to have a problem with your retriever."

"It's one of the after-lunch perks."

"It was such a darn good shot—I couldn't resist having it mounted."

"Give me a break!"

TREE
STAND
NO. 7
TROY

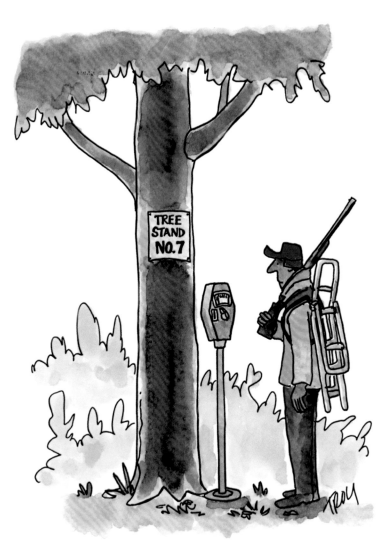

"How long have you been hunting these toxic dump sites?"

"It's part of his '08–'09 hunting season contract."

"He's been that way ever since I missed a wild boar."

"You can stop running now. We're home and the bear is still in the woods."

"If anyone gets a record buck this year, it will probably be Herb."

"Swimming is not one of his strong points."

"NO, NO, now's NOT the time to bark 'treed'!"

"He jogs with me in the off-season."

"What, remove him and ruin a perfectly good story?"

"On second thought, it does look like your bird. So can I have my dog back?"

"Nice gun, Ed. Shoots 5,000 FP of .600 Nitro Express at 100 yards, eh? What's it do at three feet?"

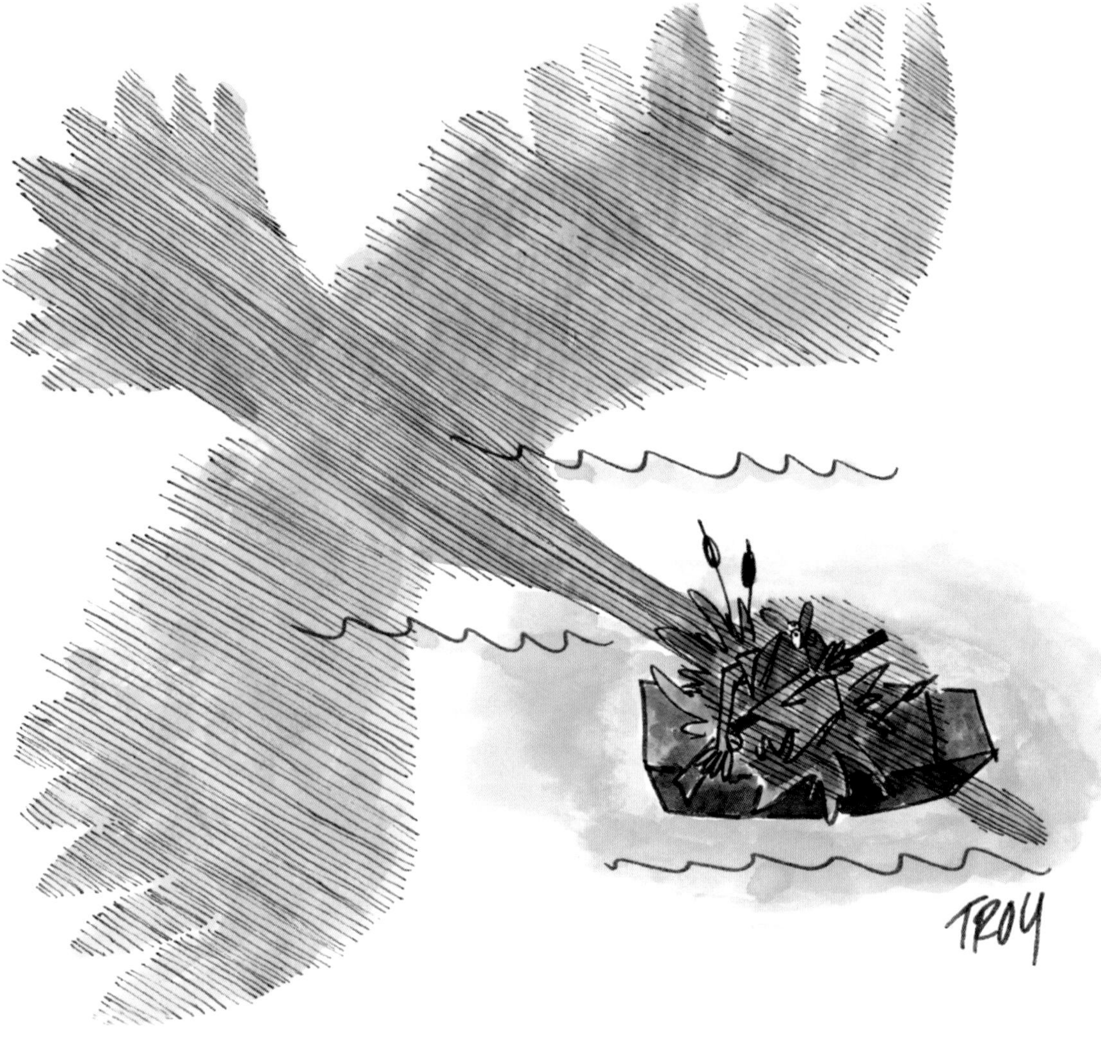
TROY

"The bear went this way. Now which way did Spot go?"

"He's been retrieving all morning. Matter of fact, it's the same duck."

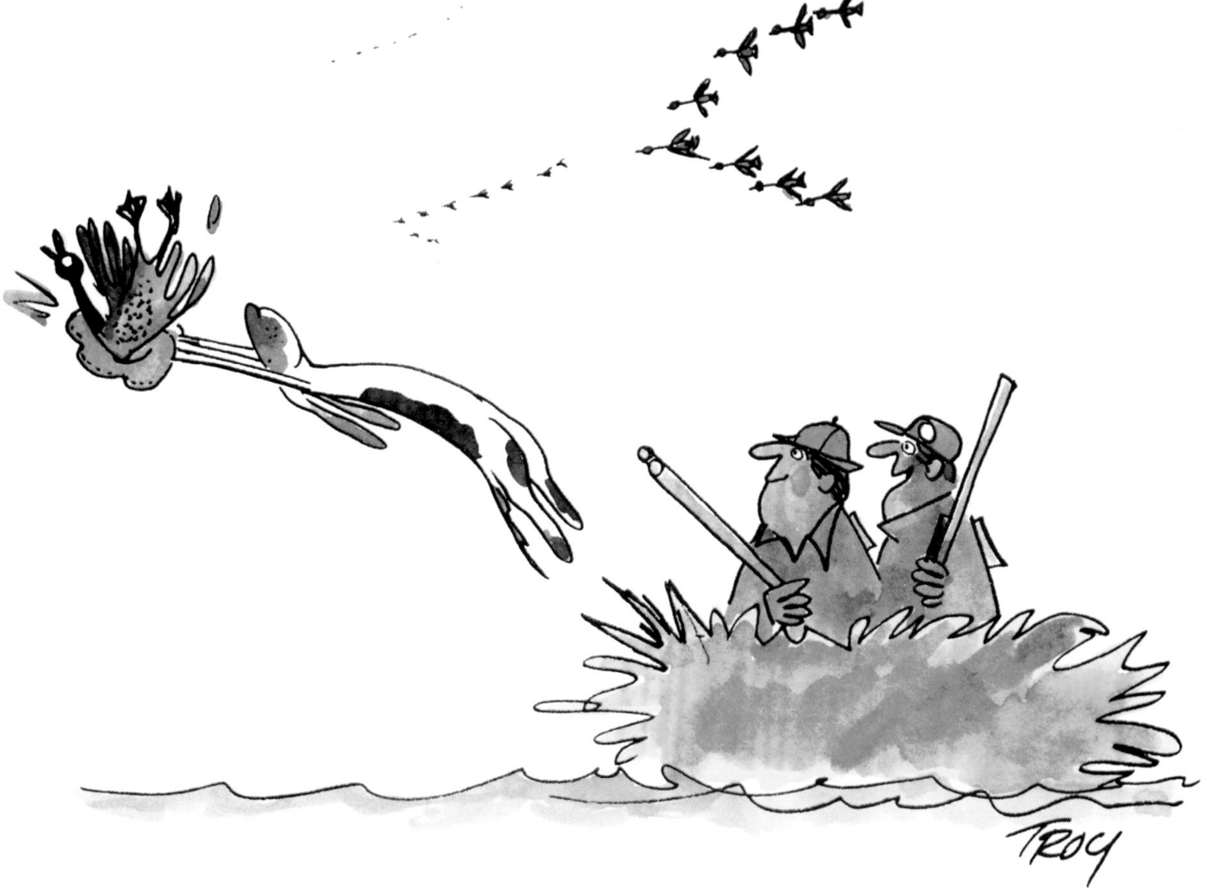
TROY

"I like his style."

"I knew I forgot something."